STO

2

Brothers and Sisters
Are Like That!

THOMAS Y. CROWELL COMPANY · NEW YORK

BROTHERS AND SISTERS ARE LIKE THAT!

STORIES TO READ TO YOURSELF

SELECTED BY
THE CHILD STUDY ASSOCIATION
OF AMERICA

ILLUSTRATED BY MICHAEL HAMPSHIRE

ACKNOWLEDGMENTS

The publishers gratefully acknowledge permission to reprint the following: "The Lucky Number" by Catherine Woolley, copyright © 1953 by *Story-A-Day*, reprinted by permission of the author; "Nicky's Sister," copyright © 1966 by Barbara Brenner, reprinted by permission of Alfred A. Knopf, Inc.; "The One in the Middle Is the Green Kangaroo," reprinted by permission of the publisher from *The One in the Middle Is the Green Kangaroo* by Judy Blume, 1962, Reilly & Lee division of Henry Regnery Company; "Big Sister and Little Sister," text copyright © 1966 by Charlotte Zolotow, reprinted by permission of Harper & Row, Publishers, and permission of The World's Work Ltd., publishers in Great Britain; "The Boy Who Couldn't Roar," reprinted from *The Boy Who Couldn't Roar* by Grace Berquist, copyright © 1960 by Abingdon Press, used by permission; "This Room Is Mine" by Betty Ren Wright, copyright © 1966 by Western Publishing Company, Inc., reprinted by permission of the publisher; "The Sunflower Garden" from *The Sunflower Garden* by Janice May Udry, copyright © 1969 by Harvey House, Inc., reprinted by permission of the Evelyn Singer Agency; "Hush, Jon!", from *Hush, Jon!* by Joan Gill, copyright © 1968 by Doubleday & Company, Inc., reprinted by permission of Doubleday & Company, Inc.; "Evan's Corner," copyright © 1967 by Elizabeth Starr Hill, reprinted by permission of Holt, Rinehart and Winston, Inc.; "Chie and the Sports Day," reprinted by permission of The World Publishing Company from *Chie and the Sports Day* by Masako Matsuno, copyright © 1965 by Masako Matsuno.

Designed by MINA BAYLIS
Manufactured in the United States of America
L.C. Card 78-158703
ISBN 0-690-16041-0
0-690-16042-9 (LB)
1   2   3   4   5   6   7   8   9   10

Selected by the
CHILD STUDY ASSOCIATION OF AMERICA

Read-to-Me Storybook
Read Me Another Story
Read Me More Stories
Read to Me Again
Holiday Storybook
Read-to-Yourself Storybook
More Read-to-Yourself Stories:
     Fun and Magic
Castles and Dragons:
     Read-to-Yourself Fairy Tales
     for Boys and Girls
Now You Can Read to Yourself
Round About the City:
     Stories You Can Read to Yourself
Pets and More Pets:
     Read-to-Yourself Stories of the City
Brothers and Sisters Are Like That!
     Stories to Read to Yourself

To the many librarians and teachers
who have helped children find pleasure in books.

Contents

Brothers and Sisters Are Like That!

The Lucky Number

by CATHERINE WOOLLEY

IT WAS a lovely Saturday morning in June. Billy and his little sister Letty were hurrying along the street.

They were going to a big party for the schoolchildren, to celebrate the end of school. The party was in the school stadium.

Billy had been up extra early, to be sure to get there on time.

Letty had been up early, too.

"You can go with me, Letty," Billy

had told her, "even if you don't go to school."

"That's a good boy," Mother had said with a smile.

Billy took Letty's hand as they went along. He quickened his step.

"Walk faster, Letty!" he said.

They were not late. There was a long line at the stadium gate.

"Hi, Billy!" That was Jimmy, a boy in Billy's class. "Want to play marbles while we're waiting?"

"Sure!" Billy said. "You stand right here, Letty."

Billy kept his eye on Letty while he played marbles. Letty was watching something farther up in the line.

The line began to move faster. Jimmy put his marbles in his pocket. Billy and Jimmy went back to their places.

Now Billy saw what Letty was looking at. She was looking at a doll that a little girl was carrying. She couldn't keep her eyes off the doll.

Letty looked at her brother. "I'm going to get a doll like that for my birthday!" she said.

Billy said nothing. Mother and Daddy worked hard. But they did not have enough money to buy Letty a big doll. Billy was afraid Letty would be disappointed.

Now they were at the stadium gate. A man handed Billy a paper bag and a ticket. He handed Letty a paper bag and a ticket.

"Keep your tickets," the man called. "You may have a lucky number."

Billy held Letty's hand tightly. They climbed the steps to the seats and sat down.

Quickly children filled the seats.

"Look, Letty," Billy said. "There's candy in your bag."

He opened the bag for her. It held small hard candies. Billy and Letty sat happily eating their candy.

A band played. They all stood up to sing "The Star-Spangled Banner."

The entertainment began. On a platform down on the field, a man juggled balls. He kept five balls spinning in the air at once. The children cheered.

A man climbed on another man's

shoulders and stood on the man's head. The children liked that, too.

Soon the entertainment was over.

Now a man stood on the platform and spoke through a microphone.

"We're going to read the lucky numbers," he said. "Prizes are only for schoolchildren."

Billy thought, "Letty can't win a prize. She won't go to school until fall."

A girl on the platform put her hand into a box and took out a ticket.

"The first lucky number," the man called, "is 106—one, oh, six. Whoever has 106 please come and get this fine prize."

He held up the prize. It was a brand-new baseball bat.

Billy looked down at his number. Number 85. "Oh," he thought, "if I could only win a baseball bat!"

A boy ran down the steps and across
the field to the stage. He gave the man
his ticket. The man handed him the baseball bat.

"Oh-h-h!" said all the children loudly.
The boy came smiling back to his seat,
carrying the bat.

The man held up a fuzzy toy dog.
He read the lucky number. A girl had

the number. She brought back the toy dog.

Then a boy won a cowboy hat.

"I wish I had a hat like that," Billy thought.

A girl won a huge rubber ball.

A boy won a baseball.

"Gee, but I'd like a baseball," Billy thought.

The man held up the next prize. It was a big doll with light curly hair and a pink dress.

"Here is a fine prize!" the man called. "Does some lucky little girl have the lucky number? The number is 85—eight, five."

Billy's heart gave a jump. He looked quickly at the ticket clutched in his hand. It was 85 all right!

"I've got it!" he cried, jumping up.

The boys around him began to laugh and hoot.

"Ha, ha! See who gets the doll!" one boy said.

"Hey, go get your dolly!" another one called.

"Look who plays with dolls, fellows!" shouted a third.

Billy sat down again.

If he went to the platform and carried back the doll, all the boys in the stadium would laugh. He couldn't do it.

Then he saw Letty. She was sitting on the edge of her seat. Her brown eyes were fastened on the doll.

For a moment Billy sat there.

"Who has 85?" the man called. "Who wins this beautiful doll?"

Slowly Billy got up. He went down the steps. He walked across the field.

In the seats the children began to laugh and whistle.

Billy climbed the steps to the platform. He held out his ticket.

"Eighty-five," the man read. "Tell the lady here your name and school."

Then the man looked at Billy. "Suppose we give you a baseball bat instead of the doll, son," he said.

Billy's heart leaped up.

Then he thought how much Letty wanted a doll.

Billy looked at the baseball bat. He looked at the doll. He took a deep breath.

"No, thanks," he said. "I'll take the doll."

He marched down the steps carrying the big doll.

Again the children whistled and laughed to see Billy carrying the doll. Billy looked straight ahead.

He was halfway to his seat when Letty came running to meet him.

Billy stopped. He gave the doll to Letty. He took Letty's hand. Together they climbed back to their seats.

The laughing and whistling died down.

Then, all through the stadium, the children began to clap their hands. They clapped them long and loud for Billy.

Nicky's Sister

by BARBARA BRENNER

ONCE there were three of them—
Father, Mother, and Nicky.

Then, one day, there were four of
them.

The fourth was a baby.

It had no hair and no teeth, and a red
face and a wet diaper.

"What do you think of her?" Mother
and Father asked Nicky.

Nicky said he wished *she* had been a
he.

Everyone came over. All the aunts

and uncles. They all came to see the baby.
It was quite bad the way they fussed over
it.

"How sweet!" said Aunt Millie.

"How cute!" said Aunt Tillie.

"Kitchy-koo!" said Uncle George.

The presents piled up and piled up.

Not for Nicky.

For the baby.

Everyone asked Nicky how he liked
the baby. He told them he would rather
have had a hamster.

"A hamster is more fun," said Nicky.

But the baby stayed.

She drank bottles and bottles of milk.

She slept and slept and slept.

And she always had a wet diaper.

She couldn't do anything.

"Won't she ever *do* anything?" asked
Nicky. "Talk or skate or play baseball?"

Nicky was disgusted.

Well, after a while, the baby did grow.

She learned to do some things. Like put her cereal bowl on her head. And she said, "gee-na-wah!"

Nicky's mother thought it was funny. Nicky didn't.

"If *I* did that, you wouldn't laugh," said Nicky. He was disgusted.

The baby got everything. She got the lamb chop with no fat. She got piggybacks.

"How come?" Nicky asked his father. "How come she gets piggybacks and I don't?"

"You're too big, pal," said his father. "But I'll tell you what I'll do. I'll play you a game of marbles."

Nicky said he'd rather have a piggy-back. Nicky was disgusted.

One day the baby got hold of Nicky's Indian. It was his best plastic Indian. She chewed it to pieces.

Nicky's mother said it was too bad. "But you see," she said to Nicky, "the baby has teeth now!"

Nicky didn't care about her teeth. He cared about his Indian. He was disgusted. Really disgusted.

Nicky made up his mind. He made up his mind to run away. He'd run away from the three of them. Then they would *really* be sorry.

Nicky went to his room. He packed his things. He packed his marbles and his baseball cards. He took his canteen. He put on his hat.

"Good-by!" he said. "I'm leaving!"

Nicky went out the back way. He went down the back steps. He started to go around to the front.

But wait! There was someone in the yard.

"Oh, it's only the silly, dumb baby," thought Nicky.

But—no! There was someone else there, too.

McGillicuddy! That no-good McGillicuddy. Biggest bully on the block. McGillicuddy! What was he doing here? Nicky just had to see.

Nicky walked over.

"So, McGillicuddy," said Nicky, "we meet again."

"So what!" said McGillicuddy.

"What are you doing in my yard, McGillicuddy?" asked Nicky.

"What's it to you?" said McGillicuddy.

"That happens to be my sister you are
standing near," said Nicky.

"Who cares!" said McGillicuddy.

"I want you to leave her alone," said
Nicky.

McGillicuddy looked at the baby.
"So, that's your sister, eh? She isn't
much, is she?"

"What do you mean by that?" asked
Nicky.

"I mean, I'd rather have a hamster any
day," said McGillicuddy.

"I wouldn't," said Nicky.

"What good is she?" said McGillicuddy. "Can she play baseball? Can she
skate? Can she talk? No! She's just a
silly, dumb baby!" And McGillicuddy
laughed a mean laugh.

The baby started to cry.

Well! Nicky got mad. Nicky got very mad. No one could talk about his sister that way. No one could make his sister cry and get away with it.

McGillicuddy was sorry he said those things. Nicky *made* him sorry.

Then Nicky patted the baby and wiped her tears. He took her into the house.

"What happened?" asked Nicky's mother.

Nicky said, "McGillicuddy."

"I see," said Nicky's mother.

"I'm staying," Nicky told his mother.

She hugged him and said she was glad.

"I have to stay," Nicky said. "She needs me."

"I think you're right," said Nicky's mother.

Nicky went to his room. He took off his hat. He unpacked his things. He put away his marbles and his baseball cards.

"She can't take care of herself," said Nicky.

"That's true," said his mother.

"Brothers and sisters should stick together," said Nicky.

"Always," said his mother. Then she smiled. "Your sister is lucky," she said, "to have a big brother like you."

Just then the baby said something. Her first word.

"Nick-y," said the baby.

"Hey!" said Nicky, "she can talk! She said my name!"

Once there were three of them—Father, Mother, and Nicky. Now there are four of them.

Nicky has a sister.

The One in the Middle Is the Green Kangaroo

by JUDY BLUME

FREDDY DISSEL had two problems. One was his older brother, Mike. The other was his younger sister, Ellen. Freddy thought a lot about being the one in the middle. But there was nothing he could do about it. He felt like the peanut-butter part of a sandwich, squeezed between Mike and Ellen.

Every year Mike got new clothes. He grew too big for his old ones. But Mike's old clothes weren't too small for Freddy. They fit him just fine.

Freddy used to have a room of his own. That was before Ellen was born. Now Ellen had a room of *her* own. Freddy moved in with Mike. Mr. and Mrs. Dissel said, "It's the boys' room." But they couldn't fool Freddy. He knew better!

Once Freddy tried to join Mike and his friends. Mike said, "Scoot, kid! You're in the way!" So Freddy tried to play with Ellen. Ellen didn't understand how to play his way. She messed up all of Freddy's things. Freddy got mad and pinched her. Ellen screamed.

"Freddy Dissel!" Mom yelled. "You shouldn't be mean to Ellen. She's smaller than you. She's just a baby!"

Ellen didn't look like a baby to Freddy. She didn't sound like a baby either. "She even goes to nursery school," Freddy thought. *"Some baby!"*

Freddy figured things would never get better for him. He would always be a great big middle nothing!

Then Freddy Dissel heard about the school play. Mike had never been in a play. Ellen had never been in a play. This was his chance to do something special. Freddy decided he would try it.

He waited two whole days before he went to his teacher. "Miss Gumber," he said, "I want to be in the school play."

Miss Gumber smiled and shook her head. "I'm sorry, Freddy," she said. "The play is being done by the fifth and sixth graders. The big boys and girls like Mike."

Freddy looked at the floor and mumbled. "That figures!" He started to walk away.

"Wait a minute, Freddy," Miss Gumber called. "I'll talk to Miss Matson anyway. She's in charge of the play. I'll find out if they need any second graders to help."

Finally Miss Gumber told Freddy that Miss Matson needed someone to play a special part. Miss Gumber said, "Go to the auditorium this afternoon. Maybe you'll get the part."

"Oh boy!" Freddy hollered.

Later he went to the auditorium. Miss Matson was waiting for him. Freddy walked right up close to her. He said, "I want to be in the play."

Miss Matson asked him to go up on

the stage and say that again in a very loud voice.

Freddy had never been on the stage. It was big. It made him feel small. He looked out at Miss Matson.

"I AM FREDDY," he shouted. "I WANT TO BE IN THE PLAY."

"Good," Miss Matson called. "Now then, Freddy, can you jump?"

What kind of question was that, Freddy wondered. Of course he could jump. He was in second grade, wasn't he? So he jumped. He jumped all around the stage—big jumps and little jumps.

When he was through, Miss Matson clapped her hands, and Freddy climbed down from the stage.

"I think you will be fine as the Green Kangaroo, Freddy," Miss Matson said. "It's a very important part."

Freddy didn't tell anyone at home about the play until dinner time. Then Freddy said, "Guess what, everyone. Guess what I'm going to be."

No one paid any attention to what Freddy was saying. They were too busy eating.

"I'm going to be in a play," Freddy said. "I'm going to be the Green Kangaroo!"

Mike choked on his potato and knocked over a whole glass of milk. Ellen laughed because Mike spilled his milk. Mr. Dissel jumped up. He patted Mike on the back to make him stop choking. Mrs. Dissel ran to get the sponge. She cleaned up the spilled milk. Freddy just sat there and smiled.

"What did you say?" Mike asked.

"I said I'm going to be in the school play. I said I'm going to be the Green Kangaroo!"

"It can't be true," Mike yelled. "You? Why would they pick you?"

Everyone settled down. Freddy told them just how he got the part. "It's really true," he said. "Just me. All by myself. The only Green Kangaroo in the play."

"That sounds wonderful," his dad said with a big smile.

And his mom kissed him right at the dinner table. "We're all proud of you, Freddy," she said.

Ellen was excited, too. She kept laughing. But Mike just shook his head and repeated, "Wow! He's going to be the Green Kangaroo!"

The next two weeks were busy ones for Freddy. He had to practice being the Green Kangaroo a lot. He practiced at school on the stage. He practiced at home, too. He made kangaroo faces in front of the mirror. He did kangaroo jumps on his bed. He even dreamed about Green Kangaroos at night.

Finally the day of the play came. The whole family and the neighbors planned to be there.

Mrs. Dissel hugged Freddy extra hard as he left for school. "We'll be there watching you, Green Kangaroo," she said.

After lunch Miss Gumber called to Freddy, "Time to go now. Time to get into your costume." Miss Gumber walked to the hall with Freddy. Then she whispered, "We'll be in the second row. Good luck."

Freddy went to Miss Matson's room. The girls in the sixth grade had made his costume. They all giggled when Miss Matson helped Freddy into it. His Green Kangaroo suit covered all of him. It even had green feet. Only his face stuck out. Miss Matson put some green dots on it.

Miss Matson laughed. "We'll wash the dots off later. Okay?"

"Okay," Freddy mumbled. He jumped over to the mirror. He looked at himself. He really felt like a Green Kangaroo.

It was time for the play to begin. Freddy waited backstage with the fifth and sixth graders who were in the play. They looked at him and smiled. He tried to smile back. But the smile wouldn't come. His heart started to beat faster. His stomach bounced up and down. He felt funny. Then Miss Matson leaned close to him. She said, "They're waiting for you, Freddy. Go ahead."

He jumped out onto the stage. He looked out into the audience. All those people were down there—somewhere. He knew they were. It was very quiet. He could hear his heart. He thought he saw his mom and dad. He thought he saw Ellen. He thought he saw Mike and his own second grade class and Miss Gumber and all of the neighbors, too. They were all out there somewhere. They were all in the middle of the audience. But Freddy wasn't in the middle. He was all by himself up on the stage. He had a job to do. He *had* to be the Green Kangaroo.

Freddy smiled. His heart slowed down. His stomach stayed still. He felt better.

He smiled a bigger, wider smile. He felt
good.

"HELLO, EVERYONE," Freddy said.

"I AM THE GREEN KANGAROO. WEL-
COME."

The play began. Freddy did his little
jumps. Every now and then one of the
fifth or sixth graders in the play said to
him, "And who are you?"

Freddy jumped around and answered,
"Me? I am the Green Kangaroo!" It was

easy. That was all he had to say. It was fun, too. Every time he said it the audience laughed. Freddy liked it when they laughed. It was a funny play.

When it was all over, everyone on the stage took a bow. Then Miss Matson came out and waited for the audience to get quiet. She said, "A special thank-you to our second grader, Freddy Dissel. He played the part of the Green Kangaroo."

Freddy jumped over to the middle of the stage. He took a big, low bow all by himself. The audience clapped hard for a long time.

Freddy didn't care much about wearing Mike's clothes any more. He didn't care much about sharing Mike's room, either. He didn't care much that Ellen was small and cute. He didn't even care much about being the one in the middle. He felt just great being Freddy Dissel.

Big Sister and Little Sister

by *CHARLOTTE ZOLOTOW*

ONCE there was a big sister and a little sister. The big sister always took care. Even when she was jumping rope, she took care that her little sister stayed on the sidewalk.

When she rode her bike, she gave her little sister a ride. When she was walking to school, she took little sister's hand and helped her cross the street. When they were playing in the fields, she made sure little sister didn't get lost.

When they were sewing, she made

sure little sister's needle was threaded and that little sister held the scissors the right way.

Big sister took care of everything, and little sister thought there was nothing big sister couldn't do.

Little sister would sometimes cry, but big sister always made her stop. First she'd put her arm around her, then she'd hold out her handkerchief and say, "Here, blow."

Big sister knew everything.

"Don't do it like that," she'd say. "Do it this way."

And little sister did. Nothing could bother big sister. She knew too much.

But one day little sister wanted to be alone. She was tired of big sister saying,

"Sit here."

"Go there."

"Do it this way."

"Come along."

And while big sister was getting lemonade and cookies for them, little sister slipped away, out of the house, out of the yard, down the road, and into the meadow, where daisies and grass hid her. Pretty soon she heard big sister calling, calling, and calling. But she didn't answer.

She heard big sister's voice getting louder when she was close and fainter when she went the other way, calling, calling.

Little sister leaned back in the daisies. She thought about lemonade and cookies. She thought about the book big sister had promised to read to her.

She thought about big sister saying,

"Sit here."

"Go there."

"Do it this way."

"Come along."

No one told little sister anything now.

The daisies bent back and forth in the sun. A big bee bumbled by.

The weeds scratched under her bare legs. But she didn't move. She heard big sister's voice coming back. It came closer and closer. And suddenly big sister was so near, little sister could have touched her.

Big sister sat down in the daisies. She stopped calling. And she began to cry. She cried just the way little sister often did.

When the little sister cried, the big one comforted her. But there was no one to put an arm around big sister. No one took out a handkerchief and said, "Here, blow." Big sister just sat there crying, alone.

Little sister stood up, but big sister didn't even see her, she was crying so completely.

Little sister went over and put her arm around big sister. She took out her handkerchief and said kindly, "Here, blow."

Big sister did. Then the little sister hugged her.

"Where have you been?" big sister asked.

"Never mind," said little sister.

"Let's go home and have some lemonade."

And from that day on little sister and big sister both took care of each other, because little sister had learned from big sister, and now they both knew how.

The Boy Who Couldn't Roar

by *GRACE BERQUIST*

Tommy watched his big brother, Keith, walk toward the field. Keith was going to John's house.

Keith and John were building a tree house. They did wonderful things together.

Sometimes Tommy wished that he could help. But Keith always said that he was too small.

"Keith," called Father, "you'd better get a sweater. And who's going for the cows this afternoon?"

"Tommy," Keith called back. "And I'll take Tommy's sweater. He can go back for another one. John is waiting for me."

Tommy started to take off his sweater.

But Father said, "Get your own sweater, Keith."

Keith looked at Father and ran to the house.

"Can you get the cows alone, Tommy?" asked Father.

"Oh, yes," said Tommy. "Keith says I'm big enough to do it alone now. He showed me how."

"Tommy, Tommy," said Father. "What am I going to do with you? You need to roar like a lion."

"How can I roar like a lion?"

"Someday you'll know," said Father. "Maybe the surprise I have for you to-morrow will help."

As Tommy walked to the pasture, he thought about the surprise. What could it be?

And he thought about the roaring. It would be fun to roar like a lion.

When he got to the pasture, he tried it.

"Roar, ROAR, R—O—A—R!"

Pansy turned and looked at him. The other cows didn't even move.

The cows knew he wasn't a lion. And Tommy knew it, too.

Tommy tried roaring again that night as he got ready for bed. But he didn't roar any better than before.

Keith laughed when he heard what Tommy was doing.

"When you can roar like a lion," he said, "you can play with John and me."

The next morning Tommy tried it once as he brushed his teeth. It did sound better then.

But he didn't have time to try it again.

Father called, "Hurry, everyone! Breakfast is ready."

The surprise! Tommy ran down the stairs.

Keith and Linda ran after him.

After breakfast Father took them all out to the barn.

"Close your eyes," he said.

The children closed their eyes. A long time went by.

And then at last Father came back.

"All right, open your eyes," he said.

"It's a horse!" Tommy cried.

"A horse for me!" said Keith. "Just like John has."

"No, a horse for all of you," said Father. "You can all three ride Shorty."

Tommy and Keith hurried to pet the horse.

"Come on, Linda," said Father. "Shorty is yours, too."

But Linda stood back and just looked.

"Oh, Daddy," said Tommy. "I never thought I would own part of a horse. Shorty is the nicest horse I ever saw."

"Let me ride first," said Keith.

"You can all ride," said Father.

He helped the boys get on. Linda did not want to ride.

"I'll watch," she said.

So Father led Shorty around the yard

with Tommy and Keith on her back.

"Take turns riding and leading
Shorty," Father said. "When you get
used to her, I'll get a bridle for you. Then
you can all ride at once."

Before Father walked away, Keith
slid off and took the rope.

"I'll lead like Father," he said. "The
head part of our horse Shorty belongs

to me. And that's the part you lead."

So Tommy stayed on, and Keith led.

Linda did not get on the horse at all. She just watched.

All morning the boys played with Shorty.

Then at noontime Keith said, "It's time to feed and water our horse."

"I'll do it," said Tommy.

"No," said Keith. "The head is mine, and the head is the part that eats."

So Tommy watched, and Keith gave Shorty some hay and some water.

When Mother called them for lunch, it was time to tie the horse in the barn.

"I will tie Shorty," said Keith.

"I'll help," said Tommy.

"No, you can watch," said Keith.

So Tommy watched while Keith tied Shorty.

Then Keith ran into the house. But

Tommy stayed and looked at the horse.

She was the surprise. And the surprise was going to help him roar like a lion.

Tommy opened his mouth and roared.

Shorty turned and looked at him. But she knew he wasn't a lion. He didn't sound like a lion at all.

Tommy walked to the house very slowly.

"Are you going to John's house this afternoon?" he asked Keith at lunch. "Are you and John going to work on your tree house?"

"No," said Keith. "I'm going to play with Shorty. You can lead, and I will ride."

"But the head belongs to you," said Tommy. "And the head is the part you lead."

"Well, you can have the head sometimes," said Keith.

So that afternoon Tommy led Shorty, and Keith rode.

It was fun to play with Keith. And it was fun to lead Shorty.

When it was time to go for the cows, Keith went with Tommy. Keith rode, and Tommy led.

Keith played that he was a cowboy.

It looked like fun to Tommy.

Three days went by. Every day Tommy led Shorty, and Keith rode.

Sometimes Tommy asked to ride, but Keith would not let him.

Every day Tommy watched while Keith fed and watered the horse. Tommy kept her part of the barn clean.

As Tommy cleaned the barn, he tried to roar like a lion. But he never sounded like one. Shorty didn't help him at all.

On the fourth day, Father got a bridle and showed the boys how to put it on.

"Let me try," said Keith.

"What about you, Tommy?" asked Father.

"Let Keith do it first," said Tommy. "After I watch him, I'll know how."

So Keith, and then Tommy, put the bridle on.

"Now let's ride," said Keith. "The head part belongs to me, so I'll sit in front and guide."

Tommy got on behind Keith.

"Tommy, when are you going to roar like a lion?" asked Father.

"How do you use the bridle?" asked Keith.

"When you want Shorty to turn to the left," Father said, "pull on the left strap. When you want her to turn right, pull on the right strap. When you want her to turn around, keep pulling on one strap. When you want her to stop, pull on both straps or say, 'Whoa!'"

After that, both Tommy and Keith rode.

Keith guided Shorty, and Tommy sat behind.

Linda still watched. But sometimes she patted the horse.

Both boys rode to get the cows now. And they both played that they were cowboys.

One day, as they came back, Keith said, "You can have Shorty's head for a while today, Tommy. You can feed and water her. John and I are going to work on our tree house."

"May I go next time?" Tommy asked.

Keith laughed. "If you can roar like a lion," he said.

So Tommy fed and watered Shorty.

He fed and watered her that day, and he did it the next day, and the next.

Each day, as he worked, he tried to

roar like a lion. He roared, and he roared. But he didn't sound like a lion at all.

And each day he thought about the horse. It was fun to have Shorty's head to feed and water. But it would be fun to have her head to guide, too. Tommy knew he could do it as well as Keith.

Then one day Linda said, "I want to ride Shorty. I am a big girl. I can ride."

Keith helped Linda get on the horse. Then he got on in front of her, and Tommy got on in back.

Keith guided Shorty across the field, and he started her up a big hill.

When the horse started up the hill, Linda held on to Keith.

But Tommy could not hold on to Linda. She was too small.

As Shorty went up the hill, Tommy slid back and back. He tried to hold on, but he could not.

All at once he slid right off, Ker-plunk!

"Whoa!" said Keith.

Tommy got up and started toward the horse.

"Climb on behind Linda again," said Keith.

Tommy looked at Shorty. And as he looked, he knew that he had something to say.

"Keith, you have had your turn guiding Shorty. It is my turn now."

Keith laughed. "Get up," he said to Shorty.

But Shorty could not go. Tommy was holding the bridle.

"Get off, Keith," said Tommy. "I can feed Shorty. I can water her. And I can keep her part of the barn clean. So I can guide her, too."

Keith did not answer.

Tommy held the bridle and looked at Keith. Tommy looked at Keith as if he were going to get off.

And at last Keith did get off.

Tommy got on the horse. He sat in front of Linda, and Keith sat behind her.

"If Shorty goes downhill," Tommy said, "you will not slide off."

But before Tommy could turn the horse around, she started up the hill. She started all by herself.

Tommy pulled on both reins and yelled, "Whoa!"

But before Shorty stopped, Keith slid off. He slid to the ground, Ker-plunk!

"Are you hurt, Keith?" Tommy called.

"No," said Keith. He got up, brushed himself off, and climbed back on the horse.

Then Tommy turned Shorty around.

As she started downhill, she opened her mouth. It looked to Tommy as if she were laughing.

Tommy guided the horse all that day.

The next day it was Keith's turn. And then it was Tommy's turn again.

"We take turns guiding," said Tommy one night at dinner.

"Tommy learned from me," said Keith.

"I didn't need to learn from you," said Tommy. "I can do some things myself. I could help you and John build a tree house if you would let me."

"Goodness, Tommy," said Father. "At last you can roar like a lion."

"I can?" asked Tommy in surprise. "I try it every day, but I don't think I sound like a lion at all."

"Why, I heard you roar just now," said Father.

Tommy thought for a minute. Then he smiled.

"Is that how a lion roars!" he said.

"Of course," said Father.

"Well," said Tommy. "Then I can roar."

Keith looked at Tommy in surprise.

"After dinner come with me," he said. "We'll get John, and we'll all work on the tree house."

This Room Is Mine

by *BETTY REN WRIGHT*

"T HIS is *my* room," said Chris. That was what she always said when she was angry with her sister, Mary.

"It's my room, too," said Mary.

"This is *my* bed," said Chris. She thumped hard on the bed. "This is *my* pillow and *my* elephant. This is *my* rug."

"It's my rug, too," said Mary. "Part of it is mine."

Chris had an idea. She found her jump rope and laid it on the floor, right down the middle of the bedroom.

"Everything on this side of the rope
is mine," she said. "The bed is mine and
the window is mine and the game box is
mine and half of the closet is mine."

"Okay," Mary replied. "Everything on this side is mine. The bookshelf is mine and the laundry bag is mine and half the closet is mine and the door is mine."

Chris put her toes close to the rope. She put her doll's toes close to the rope. Mary stood on the other side. They were so close that their noses almost touched.

"Don't breathe my air," said Chris.

"I'm breathing *my* air," said Mary.

Mother came by and peeked in the doorway. "Anybody in there want milk and cookies?" she asked.

"I do," Mary shouted. She ran out into the hall.

"I do," called Chris. She started for the door and then stopped. The door was on Mary's side of the line.

"I don't," said Chris. She went back and sat down on her bed with her doll in her lap. When her mother came by after a few minutes, she was still sitting there.

"Mary's eating chocolate cookies in the kitchen," Mother said. "Don't you want some?"

"I can't," Chris replied. "This is my side of the room. She can't walk on my side and I can't walk on hers."

Mother looked at the rope on the floor. "Oh," she said.

"I'm going to stay right here forever and ever," said Chris. "I'm going to live right here. I'm going to grow up here and never go out until I'm an old, old lady."

"I see," said Mother. "Well, I'll stop in to visit sometime."

Chris thought about what it was going to be like to stay on her side of the room forever and ever.

She would have her very own Christmas tree. On the game box. She would have her very own house. On the rug. All her children would live there with her and never step over the rope. And when company came, she would pull them up through the window in a basket.

Mary came in. She stood with her toes touching the rope.

"I'm going to the playground," she said. "We're going to jump rope. Do you want to come?"

"No," said Chris. "I'm going to stay right here forever and ever."

"You can be first jumper if you let us use your rope," said Mary. "You can use my door to go out."

Chris wondered what to do. All of a sudden she didn't feel angry anymore. She wanted to jump rope. Usually the older girls wouldn't let her jump because she was just learning.

She looked at the closet door and she remembered a way people used to get out of places.

"I know what I'll do," she said. "I'll go downstairs in the elevator."

She opened the closet door and stepped inside.

"Going down," she said.

"I want to ride in the elevator, too," said Mary.

Chris gave the door a push so that it was open on Mary's side of the rope.

"Step inside and face the front," Chris said. "Going down."

"What floor is the playground on?" asked Mary.

"First floor, out the door," Chris giggled. She stepped back into the bedroom and picked up the rope.

"I thought you were going to stay on your side of the room for ever and ever," said Mother as they ran through the kitchen.

"It got too crowded," said Chris. "I'd rather jump rope."

And she and Mary ran outside.

The Sunflower Garden
by JANICE MAY UDRY

PIPSA was a little Algonkian Indian girl who lived in the eastern part of our country. She had five brothers but no sister. All the brothers except one were older than Pipsa. He was still a baby.

Pipsa's father was proud of how well her brothers could swim.

He didn't notice how well Pipsa took care of her baby brother.

Her father was proud of how well her brothers caught fish.

He didn't notice how many berries Pipsa picked.

Her father was proud of how far out into the river her brothers could throw stones.

He didn't notice how much wood Pipsa gathered for the fires.

Her father was proud of the way her brothers had learned to trap rabbits and birds.

He didn't notice the baskets Pipsa had made.

Her father was proud of the first bows made by her brothers.

He didn't notice that now Pipsa helped her mother make their clothes from deer-skin.

Pipsa's father was like most Indian fathers. He taught his sons to do the things he could do, and he often praised them. He never thought of praising a little girl.

But Pipsa's mother was proud of her

and sometimes said, "Well done, my little Pipsa!"

Every spring, after the redbud bloomed, Pipsa helped her mother plant corn and beans and squash. How her brothers loved to eat! They seldom helped with the planting or the hoeing, however.

But Pipsa's oldest brother was now allowed to take part in the Corn Dance, which was the Indian way of asking the Great Spirit for a good corn crop.

This year, Pipsa was eager for planting time to come. All winter she had been saving some special seeds in her private little birchbark box. These were sunflower seeds she had gathered in the fall when her family had visited another village. There Pipsa had seen the big sunflowers growing, and she had tasted the delicious cakes that had been made from the seeds. One of the girls in the village had helped her gather leftover seeds. She told Pipsa that the seeds also made wonderful oil for the hair and that her father sometimes crushed the dry leaves of the sunflowers and smoked them.

Now that spring was here, Pipsa planned to have a sunflower garden. No one in Pipsa's village had ever grown sunflowers. All of the work of growing them would have to be done by Pipsa herself, because her mother had all the work she could manage to do in the big corn and bean field.

While Pipsa's brothers swam and fished and practiced with their bows and arrows, Pipsa and her mother planted and hoed the vegetables. Now that Gray Squirrel, the baby brother, was over a year old, he was no longer fastened to his cradle board, and he toddled about close to his mother and sister.

The days grew warmer and warmer. Almost the only time Pipsa could work in her sunflower patch was after supper. Since the days were longer, it was light enough for her to work then. She usually had to take Gray Squirrel with her and watch that he didn't wander away into the woods.

First Pipsa scraped away the dead leaves, the old weeds, and the sticks. Then she dug and chopped the ground with a hoe and broke up all the dirt clods. She planted the sunflower seeds on an evening when she had heard her father say it would rain before morning. As she looked down at the bare, flat ground where she had planted the seeds, she wondered if the seeds were really any good. Had she planted them right?

Would they grow? Pipsa waited and watched for a sign of green.

Finally, after twelve days, the first tiny green shoot appeared. In the next week Pipsa's garden became full of little plants reaching for the sun.

Every evening she chopped down any weed that had dared to invade the baby plants during the day. When the ground was dry, she watched the sky for rain clouds.

It was a good growing summer. By July the great sunflower heads were heavy with seeds, and it would soon be time to pick them and shake out the seeds for making cakes and oil. Pipsa had to watch Gray Squirrel constantly, because he wanted to play with the sunflower heads, and he kept trying to pull them down.

The other mothers and children often came to see and admire Pipsa's big bright flowers. One of the plants was truly a giant sunflower "tree," twice as tall as Pipsa.

As the seeds ripened, Pipsa found that some other creatures loved the sunflowers, too.

"The birds and the mice are eating all

my seeds," Pipsa told her mother sadly. She spent as much time as she could guarding the sunflowers and shooing away the birds.

One evening when Pipsa was chopping weeds away from the plants and Gray Squirrel was crawling around the big leaves, Pipsa suddenly heard something frightening. She stopped and looked quickly for her baby brother. Pipsa heard a rattlesnake!

She saw the coiled creature—the biggest snake she had ever seen! It was lying in the grass waiting for the mice that came for the seeds. Now her little brother had disturbed it. The baby didn't see the snake or know what the sound meant. Pipsa put her hand to her mouth, and then, grasping the hoe, she crept swiftly and silently toward the snake. She must kill it before it bit her brother. She had never been so afraid in all her life. What if she missed? What if she only angered the snake?

With all the force she had, Pipsa whacked downward, aiming at the back of the snake's head with the hoe. Without stopping to see if she had killed it, she hit again and again. Very frightened by this time, little Gray Squirrel scrambled to his feet.

"Run, little brother, run!" cried
Pipsa.

Gray Squirrel ran crying to his mother.

In a few minutes Pipsa's mother and
father and brothers came running. Gray
Squirrel was still crying in his mother's
arms.

Pipsa felt so weak that she had to sit
down. But beside her was the dead snake.
Her brothers were amazed at the size of

it. They praised Pipsa for her courage, and for the first time Pipsa saw admiration in their eyes. And for the first time Pipsa's father bent over her and said, "Well done, my little daughter. You are a brave child."

Pipsa was so overcome by the fright of killing the snake and by the pride in the eyes of her brothers and her father that tears came to her eyes. But she fought them back. She didn't want to spoil this moment by crying!

Her father looked around him at the sunflower garden. It was the first time he had been there.

"What are these?" he asked her, puzzled.

"They are sunflowers, Father," she told him.

"What are they for?"

Pipsa told her father that soon they

would have good little cakes from the
seeds—if she could keep the birds and
mice away long enough. And she told
him how they could make hair oil, and
how her friend's father sometimes
smoked the crushed sunflower leaves
in his pipe.

Pipsa's father asked her how soon they
could have these things. He touched the
big sunflower heads with great interest.
And then he looked again at Pipsa almost
as if he had never really seen her before.

He put his big hand on her head. "I am proud of you," he said.

The next day her father told her brothers to take turns helping Pipsa guard the sunflowers until it was time to gather the seeds.

Finally, when Pipsa said that the seeds were ripe, almost everyone came to watch her gather them.

They all followed Pipsa and her family back to their home, and they watched Pipsa pound the seeds into little cakes. She gave everyone a taste. They smiled and exclaimed at the good flavor. Pipsa told them how to make oil for more beautiful hair. She gave everyone some of the seeds so that the following spring everyone in the village could grow sunflowers.

The whole village spoke proudly of the little girl who had brought a new plant and new ideas to her people. They called her the "Sunflower Girl."

As the years went by, the Indians in Pipsa's village grew more and more sunflowers, and they never forgot to give special honor to Pipsa even after she was grown and had a little girl of her own. The people often told Pipsa's little girl how her mother had grown the first sunflowers there and had given seeds to the rest of the village.

And Pipsa's brother, Gray Squirrel, never forgot that, when he was very small, she had saved his life.

Hush, Jon!

by JOAN GILL

ONCE there was a boy named Jonathan. Most people called him Jon.

Jon lived in a small apartment house. It had five floors and a creaky old elevator. Jon lived on the fifth floor. He liked the creaky old elevator.

It reminded him of a creaky old rocket ship.

One day Jon put his space helmet on. Then he went down to the ground floor and picked up the mail for his mother.

On the way back he stopped off at the

fourth floor to see what his friend Robbie felt like doing. Robbie felt like going to the zoo. Suddenly, so did Jon.

All winter long Jon and Robbie hadn't gone to the zoo. They had gone to school. Now it was June, and they wanted to go to the zoo.

Jon remembered how much his mother had liked the zoo the summer before. He asked her to take them there.

"I can't, Jon," said his mother. "I wish I could. Maybe we can all go with your father on Saturday. But I can't go today. I have to stay at home with Samantha."

Jon frowned at Samantha. Samantha was Jon's sister. She was a baby. She was five months old, and she cried. Sometimes she ate and then she cried. Other times she cried and then she ate. When she wasn't eating, she was crying.

Crying was what Samantha did best.

Jon couldn't understand why his mother would want to spend so much time with a baby that only ate and cried. But she did.

Robbie didn't have a sister. When Robbie asked his mother to take them to the zoo, she said that she would. And off they went.

As soon as Jon and Robbie reached the zoo, they saw a man tossing fish to the sea lions. They helped him. Those sea lions jumped right out of the water and caught the fish in the air. It was fun.

Everything else was fun, too. Jon ate two ice creams and lost one balloon. So did Robbie.

And they both saw almost all the animals in the zoo. They had a wonderful day.

The next afternoon Robbie went off on a train to visit his grandmother. Jon made his own train in the living room. He rode it and chugged and whooed until his mother said, "Hush, Jon! Samantha's asleep now. Can't you ride something quieter?"

Jon rode something quieter. He rode the elevator. He rode it all alone, until an alligator joined him. It looked like a dog, but Jon was sure that it was an alligator. When the alligator left, Jon missed it.

So he took his goldfish for a ride.

After a while, the goldfish looked kind of wobbly. Jon had to carry it inside. He watched it until it unwobbled. He fed it. Then he tried to think of something quiet to do next. He couldn't.

Even after Samantha awoke, Jon couldn't think of a thing to do. Of course he ate supper when his father came home from work. And, a little later, he and his father played ball in the park. But after that, Jon just sat around till bedtime. He listened to Samantha crying and wished that Robbie was home.

The next morning Jon's mother took Samantha to the doctor for a checkup. Jon went to the zoo again, with his Aunt Martha.

Aunt Martha was nice, but she sat a lot.

The first thing that Aunt Martha saw

when they got to the zoo was a bench. She sat down.

Jon sat down, too. He had to. Aunt Martha said so. Sitting wasn't much fun. All that Jon could see from the bench were a few cages and the sea lions. And he couldn't see them clearly.

The morning lasted a long time.

When Jon finally got home, lunch was ready. He tried to eat it standing up, but his mother said that was impolite. So he ate like a sea lion instead. He threw a sandwich into the air, then tried to catch it in his mouth. He missed. His mother said that was not only impolite, that was messy.

Jon wondered why his mother never got upset at the way Samantha ate. Samantha was the messiest eater that he had ever seen, and nobody called her impolite.

After lunch Jon played with his toys. But he soon grew tired of them and decided to do something more exciting. He decided to make a magic formula.

And that's exactly what he did.

He made it in the bathtub with red ink and green ink and some perfume and some shaving lotion. He even made it fizz. He used ginger ale. It was great.

Jon's mother didn't think that it was so great. When she saw it, she sort of pushed Jon to his room and told him to stay there until he learned how to behave.

Jon stayed in his room for a long time, learning how to behave. He thought that he might stay there forever and make everybody sorry. He couldn't, though, because he heard a noise in Samantha's room. He ran to see what it was.

It was Samantha; she was crying, as

usual. When she saw Jon, she cried louder. Jon walked right over to her crib. "Hush, Samantha!" he said, and he made a horrible face.

And Samantha laughed.

Jon couldn't believe it. He made another horrible face. And Samantha laughed again.

This time Jon believed it. She was laughing. Samantha was laughing!

Jon put his finger in her hand and she

grabbed it and held it. She had strong hands—for a baby.

"Maybe," thought Jon, "now that Samantha's learned how to laugh, she won't cry as much. She seems to like laughing."

Samantha seemed to like Jon, too. She wouldn't let his finger loose.

"She wants to play," Jon said to himself. "She must be growing up."

He wondered what Samantha would be like when she really grew up. If she turned out all right, she might be fun to have around. She could go to the zoo with him. And, when Robbie was away, he'd have someone to do things with. "Why," thought Jon, "Samantha might even think of things to do."

"I guess we should keep her," he decided. "I know that she's a girl, but I could call her Sam."

Samantha let Jon's finger loose at last.

Jon skipped to the kitchen where he found his mother. He told her that he was sorry about the magic formula. "I promise never to do it again," he said.

His mother forgave him. She always did.

Then Jon asked his mother how long it would take for Sam to grow up. He did say "Sam." He wondered what his mother would do about that.

His mother smiled and gave him a cookie. She said that Sam would grow up as fast as any baby could. "Especially if you help, Jon," said his mother. "Do you think that you can?"

"I think so," said Jon.

As soon as he ate his cookie, Jon began to help Samantha grow up.

He made faces at her.

And Samantha laughed.

Evan's Corner

by *ELIZABETH STARR HILL*

Evan walked home from school slowly. He stopped in front of a pet shop.

In the window a canary sang to him from its golden cage.

"Canary bird has its own cage," Evan thought. "*I* want a place of my own."

He walked on. A bright pink flower on a windowsill caught his eye. "Flower has its own pot," he thought. "Wish *I* had a place of my own."

He kept going until he reached the

big crossing. He waited by the newsstand for the light to change.

"Paper man has his own stand," he
thought. "And I, me, myself—*I* need a
place of my own."

He crossed the noisy, busy street and
turned into the building where he lived.
He trudged up four flights of steep stairs
to the two rooms that he and his family
shared.

Soon his three sisters and his two
brothers would come home. Then his
mother, and then his father.

"Mighty lot of family," Evan thought.
"And no place to call just *mine.*"

Evan wore a door key on a string
around his neck so he could unlock the
door. Usually he was the first one home.
But today the door flew open before he
touched it.

"Surprise!" His mother stood laughing in the doorway. "Mrs. Thompson said I could leave early. I beat you home, Evan!" Mrs. Thompson was the lady his mother cleaned for.

Evan gave his mother a big hug. He liked it when she got home ahead of him. Now they could have a private talk before his brothers and sisters came in.

"Mamma, you know what I've been wishing for *hard?*" Evan burst out.

"Tell me." His mother smiled.

Evan told her the canary bird had a cage. He told her the flower had a pot. He told her the paper man had a newsstand. He ended, "And *I* want a place of my own."

His mother thought and thought. At first it seemed she might not find a way.

But then her face lighted up. "Why, of course!" she said. "It will work out just right. There are eight of us. That

means each one of us can have a corner!"

Evan jumped to his feet and clapped his hands. "Can I choose mine?"

"Yes." She nodded. "Go ahead. You have first choice, Evan."

Evan ran to every corner of the rooms.

One corner had a pretty edge of rug.
Some had nothing much. One had an
interesting crack in the wall.

But the one Evan liked best, the one
he wanted for his own, had a nice small
window and a bit of polished floor.

"This is mine," Evan said happily.
"This is my corner."

Evan's mother had no kitchen. She
shared the kitchen down the hall with
another lady. Often Evan went with her
to keep her company while she fixed
supper.

But that night he paid no attention to
the rest of the family. He sat alone and
content on the floor, in his corner.

His little brother Adam asked him, "Why you want a corner of your own, Evan?"

Evan thought for a minute. "I want a chance to be lonely."

Adam tiptoed away and left him.

When supper was ready, Evan's father came to Evan's corner.

"Stew's on the table," he told him. "You want to eat with us, Evan?"

"Please, Pa," Evan asked, "if I bring my plate here, can I eat by myself?"

"Why, sure," his father said.

So Evan fetched his plate of stew and sat down on the floor again.

His family ate at the table in the next room. From his corner, Evan could see them. He heard them talking and laughing.

At dessert time he joined them.

"Why, Evan!" His father smiled. "I thought you wanted to eat by yourself."

Evan smiled back at him. "I was lonely," he said.

After supper there were jobs to do. Evan helped clear the table. He brushed his teeth. He studied for school.

When his work was done, he sat in his corner again. He looked out the window.

The sky was almost dark. Two pigeons cooed sleepily on the window ledge.

Stars lighted up, one by one. The breeze blew cooler.

Adam came behind Evan and said softly, "Are you being lonely now?"

"No," Evan answered.

"What *are* you doing then?"

"I'm wasting time," Evan told him. "In my own way. In my own corner."

Adam asked, "Can I ever come into your corner, Evan?"

"Why don't you choose a corner of your own?" Evan said.

So Adam did. He chose the corner across the room from Evan's. He sat in it. He called, "What shall I do in my corner, Evan?"

"Whatever you like."

But Adam didn't know what to do. After a minute he left his corner. He played horse with his big sister Lucy. He sat on her back and held on to her pigtails. "Gid-yup, Lucy-horse!" he shouted. They galloped round and round the room.

Evan watched the pigeons fall asleep on the ledge. He watched the sky get darker and the stars get brighter.

Finally his father called him, "Come

out of your corner, sleepyhead! It's time for bed!"

Next morning, as soon as he woke up, Evan ran to his corner. His bit of polished floor shone as brightly as ever. His window was still fun to look through.

But Evan felt that his corner needed something more.

What could it be?

He stared at the bare walls. "I know!" he thought suddenly. "I need me a picture! And I'll make it myself!"

In school that morning Evan painted a picture of the sea. He drew big waves and a green boat.

He told his teacher, "I'm going to hang this picture in my own corner!"

"That will be lovely, Evan," his teacher said.

Evan could hardly wait to get home

after school. He ran past the pet shop.

"Canary bird!" he shouted over his shoulder, "I got a place of my own now! I'm going to hang a picture in it!"

A-skip and a-gallop, he passed the windowsill with the flowerpot.

"Listen, old pink flower," he told it, "I got a place of my own! And I made me a picture for it!"

He skidded to a stop at the corner. He waited for the light to change. He spoke

to the man at the newsstand. "Guess what, mister!"

"What, little boy?"

"I'm going to hang this picture in a place that's *just mine!*"

And he skipped and rushed and almost flew the rest of the way.

He taped the picture to the wall beside the window in his corner. He stepped back to look at it.

The green boat seemed to bob on the blue waves. It bobbed too much. Evan realized the picture was crooked.

He straightened it. Now it looked just right.

Adam came home with their biggest sister, Gloria. She always picked Adam up at the day-care center on her way home from school.

Adam's eyes shone as he saw the picture. "That's mighty pretty, Evan!" he said. "Do you think I could draw a picture for my corner?"

"Sure you could."

Adam ran off. But he could not find any paper. He had no crayons. Lucy had, but she was busy with homework now. He did not dare speak to her.

He returned to Evan.

Evan sat in his corner with his back to the room. He looked up at his picture.

Adam asked softly, "Are you being lonely, Evan?"

"No."

"Are you wasting your own time in your own way?"

"No," Evan told him.

"Well, then, what are you doing?"

"Enjoying peace and quiet," Evan said.

Adam tiptoed off.

That night Evan did not sleep well.

He lay awake in bed, thinking about his corner.

It had a nice floor and a nice window and a nice picture. But was that enough?

"No," he decided finally. "I need something more."

But what?

He remembered the pink flower in its pot. He thought, "That's it! I need a plant of my own, in my own corner."

On Saturday Evan went to the playground. He took his toothbrush glass and a spoon.

The paving of the playground was cracked. Grass and weeds grew up through the broken concrete.

Evan found a weed that had big, lacy flowers on it. He dug it up with his spoon. He planted it in his toothbrush glass.

Then he took it home and put it on the windowsill, in his own corner.

Adam came over to see what was going on. "What you doing, Evan?" he asked.

"Watching my plant grow," Evan told him.

"Maybe I'll have a plant, too, someday," Adam said softly.

Evan didn't answer. Something was bothering him.

Even now, his corner seemed not quite perfect. And he didn't know why.

"I got me no furniture," he realized

at last. "Why didn't I think of that before?"

Evan skipped off to the grocery store. He asked Mr. Meehan for two old orange crates.

"What do you want them for?" Mr. Meehan asked.

"Going to make me some furniture," Evan said proudly. "To put in a place of my own."

Mr. Meehan let him have the crates.

In his corner Evan stood one of the crates up on end. Now it was like a high desk. He turned the other crate upside down to make a bench. He sat on the bench.

Surely he had all anyone could wish for.

And yet . . .

"How come I feel like something's still missing?" Evan wondered.

He puzzled and puzzled it over. Suddenly he remembered the canary bird in its cage.

A great idea struck him: "I know! I need a pet to take care of. A pet of my own, in my own corner."

And he ran out to the pet shop.

He looked at the canary bird in the window. "Well, canary bird," he thought, "you sing fine. But you're not the pet for me."

He walked into the store. A goldfish swam over to the edge of its bowl and stared at him.

"Afternoon, Mister Fish," Evan said politely. But he thought, "No sir. That's not the pet for me."

He moved on to the turtle tank. A sign above it read, "Bargain! Special! Turtle with bowl, only 50¢!" Beside the tank a neat row of empty little bowls waited.

Evan peered into the tank. Ten or twelve lively baby green turtles swam and scrambled all over each other.

One climbed up on a rock in the middle of the water. It looked at Evan. He felt like laughing. It must have been the funniest turtle in the world!

That baby turtle had the *scrawniest* neck. Its feet were big and ugly. Its eyes were merry and black. If a turtle could smile, that turtle was smiling.

It took a dive off the rock. Clumsy turtle! It landed upside down in the shallow water! Its legs waved wildly in the air.

Evan turned it over carefully. The turtle winked at him as though it knew a secret. It looked as cheerful as ever.

"Yes sir, yes sir!" Evan told that funny little turtle joyfully. "*You're* the pet for me!"

Evan's heart beat hard and fast. He

asked the pet-shop man, "Please, mister, do you have a job a boy can do? I'd mighty much like to earn enough to buy a turtle!"

"Sorry, son, I don't need help. Try next door," the pet-shop man suggested.

Evan went next door to the Chinese bakery and asked for work. "Ah, no," Mr. Fong told him gently, "my sons help me. Try across the street."

Evan crossed the street. He marched from store to store, asking for work. He had no luck.

"Maybe some lady would pay me to carry her packages," Evan thought.

He turned in at the supermarket. He stood by the checkout counter. A lady came through. Evan asked, "Carry your bags, lady?"

She did not answer. She walked on by.

Evan waited for the next lady. This

time he smiled extra politely and spoke a little louder. "Excuse me, but those bags look mighty heavy. Carry them for you?"

"Why, yes." She put them in his arms. "That would be a big help."

Evan carried the groceries up the block to where she lived. The lady thanked him. She gave him a dime.

A dime! He had a dime! Now all he needed was four more!

Evan raced back to the supermarket. He stood by the checkout. He waited. He smiled. He spoke politely.

Lots of ladies went past. But none of them wanted him to carry her bags.

Just as Evan began to fear that he would never make another cent, a young girl said, "Oh, good! I hate lugging bundles!"

She, too, gave Evan a dime.

"Only three more to go," he thought happily.

On Sunday the supermarket was closed. But Evan went there right after school on Monday.

He made one more dime, then another. He had forty cents!

"Listen, you turtle!" he thought, "You're almost mine!"

But the next day he fooled around for

a while after school. When he finally got to the supermarket, a bigger boy was there ahead of him.

Evan's heart sank. He had supposed it would be so easy to earn only one dime! He hung around all afternoon, hoping. But the other boy got the jobs. And Evan still had only forty cents.

Next day he rushed from school to the supermarket as fast as his legs would go. Panting, he ran right to the checkout counter. The other boy was not there!

"Hurray!" Evan thought. "Bet this is my lucky day!"

At first things were slow. Then, toward closing time, a marvelous moment came. A white-haired lady spoke to him: "Sonny, do you think you could help me with these heavy groceries?"

Evan said eagerly, "Yes *ma'am!*"

Her bag was still on the counter. It

was a huge one, filled clear up to the top. Somehow Evan got his arms around it and hoisted it off the counter. "Where to, lady?" he gasped.

"Why," she said sweetly, "I live just next door." She added, "Three flights up."

Evan staggered out of the store with the bag. He followed the lady next door without much trouble. But he thought he never *would* get up those stairs.

Yet at last he made it. He eased the bag down on the lady's kitchen table.

"Thank you," she said. And she gave him the dime—the wonderful dime—the shining dime that made five!

Evan ran to the pet shop at top speed. He poured the dimes on the counter and said proudly, "I earned some money, mister! I'd like to buy me a turtle!"

The pet-shop man counted the dimes,

"All right, son. Choose one," he said.

Evan looked into the tank. His eyes passed from one shining green shell to another.

Suddenly he saw a scrawny neck stretch up from the water. A turtle rose, climbed the rock—and fell off upside down, on his back.

"This one!" Evan picked the turtle up. "This one is mine!"

Evan carried the turtle home in a small bowl. He set it on top of the upturned orange crate.

Adam was already home from the day-care center. He asked excitedly, "What you got now, Evan?"

"My own pet," Evan boasted. "To take care of, in my own corner."

Adam looked at the turtle. It winked at him cheerfully.

Adam wanted to see it closer. But he

knew he wasn't allowed in Evan's corner.

"Evan, do you think I could ever have a pet of my own?" Adam asked.

"Sure. When you're much, much older."

Adam wandered sadly away.

Now Evan had many things. He had a place of his own. He could be lonely there. He could waste time if he liked. He could enjoy peace and quiet.

He had a fine picture to look at.

He had a bench of his own to sit on, by his own window. His plant thrived and grew tall.

Best of all, he had a pet to love and take care of.

Evan spent most of his spare time in his corner. But—it was strange. He just wasn't happy.

"I must need something more," Evan thought. "But what?"

He asked his sisters. They didn't know.

He asked his brothers. They didn't know.

His father wasn't home yet. When his mother came home, Evan said, "Mama, I'm not happy in my corner. What do I need now?"

His mother put her head on one side. Together she and Evan stood off from the corner and looked at it.

Sunlight poured through the window and gleamed on the floor.

The lacy white flower stirred in a breeze.

The turtle seemed to grin through the glass of its bowl.

The painted boat rode a painted wave.

Evan's corner was beautiful. They both saw that.

"Evan," his mother said finally, "maybe what you need is to leave your corner for a while."

"Why?" Evan asked.

"Well," she said slowly, "just fixing up your own corner isn't enough." She smiled into his eyes. "Maybe you need to step out now and help somebody else."

She left him. He sat alone on his bench, thinking it over.

Adam came in. "Are you enjoying peace and quiet, Evan?" he asked.

"No," Evan said.

"What *are* you doing, then?"

Evan said slowly, "I'm planning to borrow Lucy's crayons."

"Why?"

"To help you draw a picture if you want to. I'm planning to help you fix up your corner so it's just the way you want it. I'm going to help you make it the best—

the nicest—

the very most wonderful corner in the whole world!"

Joy spread over Adam's face—and over Evan's.

They ran across the room together to work on Adam's corner.

Chie and the Sports Day

by M. MATSUNO

Some Japanese names and words you will find in this story:

Chie, pronounced *tchee-eh*

Ichiro, pronounced *ee-tchee-ro*, means *first boy*

Niichan, pronounced *nee-ee-tchan*, means *older brother*

Sushi, pronounced *soo-shee*, means *rice cakes*

Mamagoto, pronounced *mah-mah-go-toe*, means *playing house*

Yo-o-i! Don!, pronounced *yo-ee dohn*, means *Ready! Bang!* or *Ready! Go!*

"WHY should we take her? It's no fun to play with a girl," Michio said to Ichiro.

"I won't play with you if she goes with us," said Hiroshi, and the two boys ran away.

Ichiro looked back at Chie for a moment, then he, too, ran after the boys.

Chie rubbed the tears from her eyes and watched the boys disappear. Bright dragonflies flew around her head in a friendly way, but Chie was lonely.

Chie kicked a stone, and then another. The stones rolled merrily, chasing each other. But Chie had no one to chase. It seemed she was always alone these days. Kicking stones, Chie went home.

Before, Ichiro had often played *mama-goto* with Chie. He had pretended to eat the food Chie made with leaves and

flowers. And Ichiro took Chie with him on butterfly hunts.

But everything changed when Ichiro became a schoolboy. He no longer played *mamagoto* with Chie. Now, every day after school, Ichiro played with his school friends.

Once in a while, not very often, Ichiro took Chie out to play with him, and they raced. But soon Ichiro would say, "Crybaby, you're too slow," clicking his tongue. And he would run away to join his friends, just as he had today.

Chie opened the kitchen door slowly. "Chie? Is it you?" Mother called, hearing her footsteps.

But Chie didn't answer. She didn't want to see Mother. She knew just what Mother would say. "Don't cry, Chie. Ichiro will play with you tomorrow."

Always, she said the same thing, but to-morrow never came. Chie knew it wouldn't.

"Chie?" Mother called louder. "Come in, Chie, and taste this." Chie opened her eyes wide in surprise. There on the table were sandwiches, cakes, bananas and apples, chocolate candies, *sushi* . . .

"Is it a picnic?" Chie asked.

"No."

"A party?"

"No."

"What? What are these for?"

"Sports day!" Mother said merrily.

"Sports day?"

"Yes. Ichiro's sports day at school to-morrow. Didn't he tell you about it?"

"No, nothing. Can I go?"

"Yes," Mother answered, busily cut-ting more sandwiches. "You and I are going tomorrow."

"Tomorrow! Oh, tomorrow!" Chie cried, and skipped for joy.

Ichiro, too, was surprised to see the splendid lunch when he came in from play.

"It's for sports day tomorrow," Mother explained.

"But why three lunches?"

"One for me," said Chie excitedly.

"And for me, too," Mother added, smiling at Ichiro.

"But you said you couldn't come! You said you had to attend an important meeting!"

"Yes, but I'll cut it short. It's your first sports day. I want to be there," said Mother.

"And me, too," Chie cried.

Ichiro looked at Chie. Then, without a word, he turned and ran to his room.

The whole house shook as Ichiro slammed the door and threw himself on the floor. Chie was coming to the sports day. No, he couldn't bear it. "It will be awful," Ichiro thought bitterly. "She will see me running last. Last!"

Always, when Ichiro and Chie raced together, Ichiro won. "Ichiro-*Niichan* is so fast," Chie would say admiringly. But at school Ichiro was almost always the slowest runner of his class. Chie did not know it. Ichiro didn't want Chie to know it. He wanted to keep it secret. He didn't care if anyone else knew he was a slow runner. But not Chie. "She shouldn't come," said Ichiro, thumping his feet. "No, she shouldn't. Oh, I hope Mother can't get there in time."

Sports day was a beautiful autumn day. The music of the opening march soared into the deep blue October sky, and under the gay buntings girls danced.

"All first-grade boys! Fall in at the

starting gate!" called the teacher of athletics over the microphone.

"Please, please . . ." Ichiro prayed to himself as he took his place, "don't let them be here yet." His eyes searched the crowd. No, he didn't see them. Goody, they couldn't make it! Ichiro smiled secretly.

The first-grade boys were divided into groups.

"*Yo-o-i! Don!!*" (Ready! Go!!) The first group ran!

"*Yo-o-i! Don!!*" The second group ran!

Now! "*Yo-o-i! Don!!*" The third group ran! Ichiro ran!

Ichiro forgot all about Mother and Chie. He ran as he had never run before. But soon everyone in his group was ahead of him. He was slow as usual. "No matter," said Ichiro to himself, running.

"No Mother, no Chie, no Mother, no Chie . . ."

The yellow tape for the next group was already up when, his heart beating fast, he ran through the goal.

"Ichiro–*Niichan!*"

"Ichiro!"

Mother and Chie! They had just come in!

"You were the first, *Niichan!*" Chie called to her brother.

"No! Last!" Ichiro shouted.

"Last?" Chie was puzzled.

"Yes! Last!" And, seizing his lunch box, Ichiro ran away to join his friends.

During all of lunch time Ichiro stayed away from Mother and Chie.

The obstacle races began in the afternoon. Anyone who chose could join these games. Barrels, ladders, nets, and other obstacles were placed on the course, and near the end were scattered slips of paper. After a racer cleared all the other obstacles, the words on his slip told him what to do next: "Get a yellow cap" or "Find a man's shoe" or "Tie this rope."

Look! People burst into laughter. Over

there, a fat man was caught in a ladder. He began running with it around his stomach.

Ichiro enjoyed obstacle races. It was nothing for him to creep under a net or crawl through a ladder. He picked up his slip of paper. "Find a little girl and run three-legged with her," it read.

"Chie! Chie, come quickly!" Ichiro stopped right in front of Chie's seat.

"What is it? What's wrong?" asked Mother in a worried voice.

"I need a little girl to run with me three-legged."

"*Me?* Not me?"

"Yes, you!"

"Oh yes, I'll go with you!" Chie ran to her brother. "Hurry, hurry, Ichiro-*Niichan!*"

Ichiro quickly tied his right foot to Chie's left foot with his headband. One, two . . . one, two . . . Carefully the two started.

Now, faster! One, two; one, two; one, two; one, two; one—

Ah! Ichiro stumbled and fell, dragging Chie with him to the ground. Red blood ran on her knees.

"Oh . . ." Ichiro exclaimed. Now they would be out of the race. Chie would cry and run back to Mother.

"Hurry! Let's go! *Niichan,* please hurry!" Chie pulled Ichiro's hand.

Together Chie and Ichiro ran. One, two; one, two . . . Left, right; left, right . . . One, two; one, two . . . They ran and ran. And it was not until he was untying their feet at the end of the course that Ichiro realized they were first.

"Tra-ra-ra . . ." The music began again, and Ichiro and Chie walked together proudly to receive the first prize.

It was only then, at the retiring gate, that Chie noticed her bloody knees. Tears welled up in her eyes.

"Come," said Ichiro. He carried Chie on his back to the nurse.

"Does it hurt?"

"No, not much."

Outside, the sun seemed even brighter than before. Ichiro walked slowly for Chie's sake.

"You won. You won first prize!" said Chie, looking up at Ichiro.

"I? No, we!" Ichiro replied, smiling. "Half of the prize is yours. Take these notebooks and pencils. And you can have the whole box of crayons."

"Really?"

"Yes, really."

Chie was very, very happy. "Look, Mother," she called, "my notebooks, my pencils, and a whole box of crayons! I ran with Ichiro-*Niichan*, and we were first."

And Ichiro was happy, too. Why? Because he won first prize, of course. But not only because of that. Can you guess why?

"Tra-ra-ra . . ." the music was still playing. Ichiro skipped to the music to meet his friends. It was a beautiful autumn day. A deep blue October sky and bright golden sunshine. Bang! Bang! Up went the firecrackers. Bang! Bang! Bang! The games went on.

About the Child Study Association of America

The Child Study Association of America is a national, nonprofit agency, founded in 1888 to further the education of adults in all that pertains to the well-being of children. Its program emphasizes improving the quality of family life in all kinds of communities and training other members of the helping professions who work with parents and young people. The Association also publishes readable, informative books and pamphlets on various aspects of child care.

The Children's Book Committee of the Association carefully reviews all books published for children. It issues an annual list for the guidance of parents, and others with similar responsibilities, in selecting books for children. This story collection, and many others, welcomed by parents and children alike, has grown out of the committee's long years of experience in reviewing and evaluating books for children of all ages.

About the Illustrator

After a childhood on England's Yorkshire moors, Michael Hampshire studied art at the University of Leeds. He settled in the United States and later taught stage design at Marymount College in Tarrytown, New York. Mr. Hampshire is an experienced traveler, having journeyed through most of Europe as well as Ethiopia, the Sudan, Egypt, India, and Ceylon. The illustrator of many books for children, Mr. Hampshire is also an enthusiastic amateur archaeologist.